Wine Name ______________________

Winery ______________ Region ______________

Grapes ______________ Vintage ______________ Alcohol % __________

Appearance		☆ ☆ ☆ ☆ ☆
Aroma		☆ ☆ ☆ ☆ ☆
Body		☆ ☆ ☆ ☆ ☆
Taste		☆ ☆ ☆ ☆ ☆
Finish		☆ ☆ ☆ ☆ ☆

Pairs With	Serving Temperature

Notes

Ratings ☆ ☆ ☆ ☆ ☆

Wine Name ______________________________

Winery ____________________ Region ____________________

Grapes ____________________ Vintage ____________________ Alcohol % __________

Appearance		☆ ☆ ☆ ☆ ☆
Aroma		☆ ☆ ☆ ☆ ☆
Body		☆ ☆ ☆ ☆ ☆
Taste		☆ ☆ ☆ ☆ ☆
Finish		☆ ☆ ☆ ☆ ☆

Pairs With	Serving Temperature

Notes

Ratings ☆ ☆ ☆ ☆ ☆

Wine Name ______________________

Winery ______________ Region ______________

Grapes ______________ Vintage ______________ Alcohol % ________

Appearance		☆ ☆ ☆ ☆ ☆
Aroma		☆ ☆ ☆ ☆ ☆
Body		☆ ☆ ☆ ☆ ☆
Taste		☆ ☆ ☆ ☆ ☆
Finish		☆ ☆ ☆ ☆ ☆

Pairs With	Serving Temperature

Notes

Ratings ☆ ☆ ☆ ☆ ☆

Wine Name ______________________

Winery ______________ Region ______________

Grapes ______________ Vintage ______________ Alcohol % __________

Appearance		☆ ☆ ☆ ☆ ☆
Aroma		☆ ☆ ☆ ☆ ☆
Body		☆ ☆ ☆ ☆ ☆
Taste		☆ ☆ ☆ ☆ ☆
Finish		☆ ☆ ☆ ☆ ☆

Pairs With	Serving Temperature

Notes

Ratings ☆ ☆ ☆ ☆ ☆

Wine Name ______________________

Winery ______________ Region ______________

Grapes ______________ Vintage ______________ Alcohol % __________

Appearance		☆ ☆ ☆ ☆ ☆
Aroma		☆ ☆ ☆ ☆ ☆
Body		☆ ☆ ☆ ☆ ☆
Taste		☆ ☆ ☆ ☆ ☆
Finish		☆ ☆ ☆ ☆ ☆

Pairs With	Serving Temperature

Notes

Ratings ☆ ☆ ☆ ☆ ☆

Wine Name ______________________

Winery ____________ Region ____________

Grapes ____________ Vintage ____________ Alcohol % ________

Appearance		☆ ☆ ☆ ☆ ☆
Aroma		☆ ☆ ☆ ☆ ☆
Body		☆ ☆ ☆ ☆ ☆
Taste		☆ ☆ ☆ ☆ ☆
Finish		☆ ☆ ☆ ☆ ☆

Pairs With	Serving Temperature

Notes

Ratings ☆ ☆ ☆ ☆ ☆

Wine Name

Winery _______________ Region _______________

Grapes _______________ Vintage _______________ Alcohol % _______________

Appearance		☆ ☆ ☆ ☆ ☆
Aroma		☆ ☆ ☆ ☆ ☆
Body		☆ ☆ ☆ ☆ ☆
Taste		☆ ☆ ☆ ☆ ☆
Finish		☆ ☆ ☆ ☆ ☆

Pairs With	Serving Temperature

Notes

Ratings ☆ ☆ ☆ ☆ ☆

Wine Name ______________________

Winery ______________ Region ______________

Grapes ______________ Vintage ______________ Alcohol % __________

Appearance		☆ ☆ ☆ ☆ ☆
Aroma		☆ ☆ ☆ ☆ ☆
Body		☆ ☆ ☆ ☆ ☆
Taste		☆ ☆ ☆ ☆ ☆
Finish		☆ ☆ ☆ ☆ ☆

Pairs With	Serving Temperature

Notes

Ratings ☆ ☆ ☆ ☆ ☆

Wine Name ______________________

Winery ______________ Region ______________

Grapes ______________ Vintage ______________ Alcohol % __________

Appearance		☆ ☆ ☆ ☆ ☆
Aroma		☆ ☆ ☆ ☆ ☆
Body		☆ ☆ ☆ ☆ ☆
Taste		☆ ☆ ☆ ☆ ☆
Finish		☆ ☆ ☆ ☆ ☆

Pairs With	Serving Temperature

Notes

Ratings ☆ ☆ ☆ ☆ ☆

Wine Name ______________________

Winery ______________ Region ______________

Grapes ______________ Vintage ______________ Alcohol % __________

Appearance		☆ ☆ ☆ ☆ ☆
Aroma		☆ ☆ ☆ ☆ ☆
Body		☆ ☆ ☆ ☆ ☆
Taste		☆ ☆ ☆ ☆ ☆
Finish		☆ ☆ ☆ ☆ ☆

Pairs With	Serving Temperature

Notes

Ratings ☆ ☆ ☆ ☆ ☆

Wine Name ______________________

Winery ______________ Region ______________

Grapes ______________ Vintage ______________ Alcohol % ________

Appearance		☆ ☆ ☆ ☆ ☆
Aroma		☆ ☆ ☆ ☆ ☆
Body		☆ ☆ ☆ ☆ ☆
Taste		☆ ☆ ☆ ☆ ☆
Finish		☆ ☆ ☆ ☆ ☆

Pairs With	Serving Temperature

Notes

Ratings ☆ ☆ ☆ ☆ ☆

Wine Name ______________________

Winery ____________ Region ____________

Grapes ____________ Vintage ____________ Alcohol % ____________

Appearance		☆ ☆ ☆ ☆ ☆
Aroma		☆ ☆ ☆ ☆ ☆
Body		☆ ☆ ☆ ☆ ☆
Taste		☆ ☆ ☆ ☆ ☆
Finish		☆ ☆ ☆ ☆ ☆

Pairs With	Serving Temperature

Notes

Ratings ☆ ☆ ☆ ☆ ☆

Wine Name

Winery ____________ Region ____________

Grapes ____________ Vintage ____________ Alcohol % ____________

Appearance		
Aroma		
Body		
Taste		
Finish		

Pairs With	Serving Temperature

Notes

Ratings

Wine Name ______

Winery ______ Region ______

Grapes ______ Vintage ______ Alcohol % ______

Appearance		☆ ☆ ☆ ☆ ☆
Aroma		☆ ☆ ☆ ☆ ☆
Body		☆ ☆ ☆ ☆ ☆
Taste		☆ ☆ ☆ ☆ ☆
Finish		☆ ☆ ☆ ☆ ☆

Pairs With	Serving Temperature

Notes

Ratings ☆ ☆ ☆ ☆ ☆

Wine Name ______________________

Winery ______________ Region ______________

Grapes ______________ Vintage ______________ Alcohol % ________

Appearance		☆ ☆ ☆ ☆ ☆
Aroma		☆ ☆ ☆ ☆ ☆
Body		☆ ☆ ☆ ☆ ☆
Taste		☆ ☆ ☆ ☆ ☆
Finish		☆ ☆ ☆ ☆ ☆

Pairs With	Serving Temperature

Notes

Ratings ☆ ☆ ☆ ☆ ☆

Wine Name

Winery ______________ Region ______________

Grapes ______________ Vintage ______________ Alcohol % ______________

Appearance		☆ ☆ ☆ ☆ ☆
Aroma		☆ ☆ ☆ ☆ ☆
Body		☆ ☆ ☆ ☆ ☆
Taste		☆ ☆ ☆ ☆ ☆
Finish		☆ ☆ ☆ ☆ ☆

Pairs With	Serving Temperature

Notes

Ratings ☆ ☆ ☆ ☆ ☆

Wine Name ________________

Winery ________________ Region ________________

Grapes ________________ Vintage ________________ Alcohol % ________

Appearance		☆ ☆ ☆ ☆ ☆
Aroma		☆ ☆ ☆ ☆ ☆
Body		☆ ☆ ☆ ☆ ☆
Taste		☆ ☆ ☆ ☆ ☆
Finish		☆ ☆ ☆ ☆ ☆

Pairs With	Serving Temperature

Notes

Ratings ☆ ☆ ☆ ☆ ☆

Wine Name ______________________

Winery ____________ Region ____________

Grapes ____________ Vintage ____________ Alcohol % ________

Appearance		☆ ☆ ☆ ☆ ☆
Aroma		☆ ☆ ☆ ☆ ☆
Body		☆ ☆ ☆ ☆ ☆
Taste		☆ ☆ ☆ ☆ ☆
Finish		☆ ☆ ☆ ☆ ☆

Pairs With	Serving Temperature

Notes

Ratings ☆ ☆ ☆ ☆ ☆

Wine Name ______________________

Winery ______________ Region ______________

Grapes ______________ Vintage ______________ Alcohol % ________

Appearance		☆ ☆ ☆ ☆ ☆
Aroma		☆ ☆ ☆ ☆ ☆
Body		☆ ☆ ☆ ☆ ☆
Taste		☆ ☆ ☆ ☆ ☆
Finish		☆ ☆ ☆ ☆ ☆

Pairs With	Serving Temperature

Notes

Ratings ☆ ☆ ☆ ☆ ☆

Wine Name

Winery Region

Grapes Vintage Alcohol %

Appearance		☆ ☆ ☆ ☆ ☆
Aroma		☆ ☆ ☆ ☆ ☆
Body		☆ ☆ ☆ ☆ ☆
Taste		☆ ☆ ☆ ☆ ☆
Finish		☆ ☆ ☆ ☆ ☆

Pairs With	Serving Temperature

Notes

Ratings ☆ ☆ ☆ ☆ ☆

Wine Name

Winery ____________ Region ____________

Grapes ____________ Vintage ____________ Alcohol % ____________

Appearance		☆ ☆ ☆ ☆ ☆
Aroma		☆ ☆ ☆ ☆ ☆
Body		☆ ☆ ☆ ☆ ☆
Taste		☆ ☆ ☆ ☆ ☆
Finish		☆ ☆ ☆ ☆ ☆

Pairs With	Serving Temperature

Notes

Ratings ☆ ☆ ☆ ☆ ☆

Wine Name ____________________

Winery ____________ Region ____________

Grapes ____________ Vintage ____________ Alcohol % ________

Appearance		☆ ☆ ☆ ☆ ☆
Aroma		☆ ☆ ☆ ☆ ☆
Body		☆ ☆ ☆ ☆ ☆
Taste		☆ ☆ ☆ ☆ ☆
Finish		☆ ☆ ☆ ☆ ☆

Pairs With	Serving Temperature

Notes

Ratings ☆ ☆ ☆ ☆ ☆

Wine Name ______________________

Winery ______________ Region ______________

Grapes ______________ Vintage ______________ Alcohol % ________

Appearance		☆ ☆ ☆ ☆ ☆
Aroma		☆ ☆ ☆ ☆ ☆
Body		☆ ☆ ☆ ☆ ☆
Taste		☆ ☆ ☆ ☆ ☆
Finish		☆ ☆ ☆ ☆ ☆

Pairs With	Serving Temperature

Notes

Ratings ☆ ☆ ☆ ☆ ☆

Wine Name ______________________________

Winery ______________ Region ______________

Grapes ______________ Vintage ______________ Alcohol % ________

Appearance		☆ ☆ ☆ ☆ ☆
Aroma		☆ ☆ ☆ ☆ ☆
Body		☆ ☆ ☆ ☆ ☆
Taste		☆ ☆ ☆ ☆ ☆
Finish		☆ ☆ ☆ ☆ ☆

Pairs With	Serving Temperature

Notes

Ratings ☆ ☆ ☆ ☆ ☆

Wine Name ____________________

Winery ____________ Region ____________

Grapes ____________ Vintage ____________ Alcohol % ________

Appearance		☆ ☆ ☆ ☆ ☆
Aroma		☆ ☆ ☆ ☆ ☆
Body		☆ ☆ ☆ ☆ ☆
Taste		☆ ☆ ☆ ☆ ☆
Finish		☆ ☆ ☆ ☆ ☆

Pairs With	Serving Temperature

Notes

Ratings ☆ ☆ ☆ ☆ ☆

Wine Name ____________________

Winery ____________ Region ____________

Grapes ____________ Vintage ____________ Alcohol % ________

Appearance		☆ ☆ ☆ ☆ ☆
Aroma		☆ ☆ ☆ ☆ ☆
Body		☆ ☆ ☆ ☆ ☆
Taste		☆ ☆ ☆ ☆ ☆
Finish		☆ ☆ ☆ ☆ ☆

Pairs With	Serving Temperature

Notes

Ratings ☆ ☆ ☆ ☆ ☆

Wine Name ____________________

Winery ____________________ Region ____________________

Grapes ____________________ Vintage ____________________ Alcohol % __________

Appearance		☆ ☆ ☆ ☆ ☆
Aroma		☆ ☆ ☆ ☆ ☆
Body		☆ ☆ ☆ ☆ ☆
Taste		☆ ☆ ☆ ☆ ☆
Finish		☆ ☆ ☆ ☆ ☆

Pairs With	Serving Temperature

Notes

Ratings ☆ ☆ ☆ ☆ ☆

Wine Name

Winery ____________ Region ____________

Grapes ____________ Vintage ____________ Alcohol % ____________

Appearance		☆ ☆ ☆ ☆ ☆
Aroma		☆ ☆ ☆ ☆ ☆
Body		☆ ☆ ☆ ☆ ☆
Taste		☆ ☆ ☆ ☆ ☆
Finish		☆ ☆ ☆ ☆ ☆

Pairs With	Serving Temperature

Notes

Ratings ☆ ☆ ☆ ☆ ☆

Wine Name ______________________

Winery ____________ Region ____________

Grapes ____________ Vintage ____________ Alcohol % ________

Appearance		☆ ☆ ☆ ☆ ☆
Aroma		☆ ☆ ☆ ☆ ☆
Body		☆ ☆ ☆ ☆ ☆
Taste		☆ ☆ ☆ ☆ ☆
Finish		☆ ☆ ☆ ☆ ☆

Pairs With	Serving Temperature

Notes

Ratings ☆ ☆ ☆ ☆ ☆

Wine Name ____________________

Winery ____________ Region ____________

Grapes ____________ Vintage ____________ Alcohol % ________

Appearance		☆ ☆ ☆ ☆ ☆
Aroma		☆ ☆ ☆ ☆ ☆
Body		☆ ☆ ☆ ☆ ☆
Taste		☆ ☆ ☆ ☆ ☆
Finish		☆ ☆ ☆ ☆ ☆

Pairs With	Serving Temperature

Notes

Ratings ☆ ☆ ☆ ☆ ☆

Wine Name

Winery ____________ Region ____________

Grapes ____________ Vintage ____________ Alcohol % ________

Appearance		☆ ☆ ☆ ☆ ☆
Aroma		☆ ☆ ☆ ☆ ☆
Body		☆ ☆ ☆ ☆ ☆
Taste		☆ ☆ ☆ ☆ ☆
Finish		☆ ☆ ☆ ☆ ☆

Pairs With	Serving Temperature

Notes

Ratings ☆ ☆ ☆ ☆ ☆

Wine Name ______________________

Winery ____________ Region ____________

Grapes ____________ Vintage ____________ Alcohol % ________

Appearance		☆ ☆ ☆ ☆ ☆
Aroma		☆ ☆ ☆ ☆ ☆
Body		☆ ☆ ☆ ☆ ☆
Taste		☆ ☆ ☆ ☆ ☆
Finish		☆ ☆ ☆ ☆ ☆

Pairs With	Serving Temperature

Notes

Ratings ☆ ☆ ☆ ☆ ☆

Wine Name ____________________

Winery ____________ Region ____________

Grapes ____________ Vintage ____________ Alcohol % ________

Appearance		☆ ☆ ☆ ☆ ☆
Aroma		☆ ☆ ☆ ☆ ☆
Body		☆ ☆ ☆ ☆ ☆
Taste		☆ ☆ ☆ ☆ ☆
Finish		☆ ☆ ☆ ☆ ☆

Pairs With	Serving Temperature

Notes

Ratings ☆ ☆ ☆ ☆ ☆

Wine Name ____________________

Winery ____________ Region ____________

Grapes ____________ Vintage ____________ Alcohol % ________

Appearance		☆ ☆ ☆ ☆ ☆
Aroma		☆ ☆ ☆ ☆ ☆
Body		☆ ☆ ☆ ☆ ☆
Taste		☆ ☆ ☆ ☆ ☆
Finish		☆ ☆ ☆ ☆ ☆

Pairs With	Serving Temperature

Notes

Ratings ☆ ☆ ☆ ☆ ☆

Wine Name ____________________

Winery ____________ Region ____________

Grapes ____________ Vintage ____________ Alcohol % ________

Appearance		☆ ☆ ☆ ☆ ☆
Aroma		☆ ☆ ☆ ☆ ☆
Body		☆ ☆ ☆ ☆ ☆
Taste		☆ ☆ ☆ ☆ ☆
Finish		☆ ☆ ☆ ☆ ☆

Pairs With	Serving Temperature

Notes

Ratings ☆ ☆ ☆ ☆ ☆

Wine Name ______________________

Winery ____________ Region ____________

Grapes ____________ Vintage ____________ Alcohol % ________

Appearance		☆ ☆ ☆ ☆ ☆
Aroma		☆ ☆ ☆ ☆ ☆
Body		☆ ☆ ☆ ☆ ☆
Taste		☆ ☆ ☆ ☆ ☆
Finish		☆ ☆ ☆ ☆ ☆

Pairs With	Serving Temperature

Notes

Ratings ☆ ☆ ☆ ☆ ☆

Wine Name

Winery | Region

Grapes | Vintage | Alcohol %

Appearance		☆ ☆ ☆ ☆ ☆
Aroma		☆ ☆ ☆ ☆ ☆
Body		☆ ☆ ☆ ☆ ☆
Taste		☆ ☆ ☆ ☆ ☆
Finish		☆ ☆ ☆ ☆ ☆

Pairs With	Serving Temperature

Notes

Ratings ☆ ☆ ☆ ☆ ☆

Wine Name ______________________

Winery ______________ Region ______________

Grapes ______________ Vintage ______________ Alcohol % ______________

Appearance		☆ ☆ ☆ ☆ ☆
Aroma		☆ ☆ ☆ ☆ ☆
Body		☆ ☆ ☆ ☆ ☆
Taste		☆ ☆ ☆ ☆ ☆
Finish		☆ ☆ ☆ ☆ ☆

Pairs With	Serving Temperature

Notes

Ratings ☆ ☆ ☆ ☆ ☆

Wine Name ____________________

Winery ____________ Region ____________

Grapes ____________ Vintage ____________ Alcohol % ________

Appearance		☆ ☆ ☆ ☆ ☆
Aroma		☆ ☆ ☆ ☆ ☆
Body		☆ ☆ ☆ ☆ ☆
Taste		☆ ☆ ☆ ☆ ☆
Finish		☆ ☆ ☆ ☆ ☆

Pairs With	Serving Temperature

Notes

Ratings ☆ ☆ ☆ ☆ ☆

Wine Name ______________________

Winery ______________ Region ______________

Grapes ______________ Vintage ______________ Alcohol % ______________

Appearance		☆ ☆ ☆ ☆ ☆
Aroma		☆ ☆ ☆ ☆ ☆
Body		☆ ☆ ☆ ☆ ☆
Taste		☆ ☆ ☆ ☆ ☆
Finish		☆ ☆ ☆ ☆ ☆

Pairs With	Serving Temperature

Notes

Ratings ☆ ☆ ☆ ☆ ☆

Wine Name ____________________

Winery ____________ Region ____________

Grapes ____________ Vintage ____________ Alcohol % ________

Appearance		☆☆☆☆☆
Aroma		☆☆☆☆☆
Body		☆☆☆☆☆
Taste		☆☆☆☆☆
Finish		☆☆☆☆☆

Pairs With	Serving Temperature

Notes

Ratings ☆☆☆☆☆

Wine Name ______________________

Winery ______________ Region ______________

Grapes ______________ Vintage ______________ Alcohol % ________

Appearance		☆ ☆ ☆ ☆ ☆
Aroma		☆ ☆ ☆ ☆ ☆
Body		☆ ☆ ☆ ☆ ☆
Taste		☆ ☆ ☆ ☆ ☆
Finish		☆ ☆ ☆ ☆ ☆

Pairs With	Serving Temperature

Notes

Ratings ☆ ☆ ☆ ☆ ☆

Wine Name

Winery ______________ Region ______________

Grapes ______________ Vintage ______________ Alcohol % ________

Appearance		☆ ☆ ☆ ☆ ☆
Aroma		☆ ☆ ☆ ☆ ☆
Body		☆ ☆ ☆ ☆ ☆
Taste		☆ ☆ ☆ ☆ ☆
Finish		☆ ☆ ☆ ☆ ☆

Pairs With	Serving Temperature

Notes

Ratings ☆ ☆ ☆ ☆ ☆

Wine Name

Winery Region

Grapes Vintage Alcohol %

Appearance		☆ ☆ ☆ ☆ ☆
Aroma		☆ ☆ ☆ ☆ ☆
Body		☆ ☆ ☆ ☆ ☆
Taste		☆ ☆ ☆ ☆ ☆
Finish		☆ ☆ ☆ ☆ ☆

Pairs With	Serving Temperature

Notes

Ratings ☆ ☆ ☆ ☆ ☆

Wine Name ______________________

Winery ____________ Region ____________

Grapes ____________ Vintage ____________ Alcohol % ________

Appearance		☆ ☆ ☆ ☆ ☆
Aroma		☆ ☆ ☆ ☆ ☆
Body		☆ ☆ ☆ ☆ ☆
Taste		☆ ☆ ☆ ☆ ☆
Finish		☆ ☆ ☆ ☆ ☆

Pairs With	Serving Temperature

Notes

Ratings ☆ ☆ ☆ ☆ ☆

Wine Name ______________________

Winery ____________ Region ____________

Grapes ____________ Vintage ____________ Alcohol % ________

Appearance		☆ ☆ ☆ ☆ ☆
Aroma		☆ ☆ ☆ ☆ ☆
Body		☆ ☆ ☆ ☆ ☆
Taste		☆ ☆ ☆ ☆ ☆
Finish		☆ ☆ ☆ ☆ ☆

Pairs With	Serving Temperature

Notes

Ratings ☆ ☆ ☆ ☆ ☆

Wine Name ____________________

Winery ______________ Region ______________

Grapes ______________ Vintage ______________ Alcohol % __________

Appearance		☆ ☆ ☆ ☆ ☆
Aroma		☆ ☆ ☆ ☆ ☆
Body		☆ ☆ ☆ ☆ ☆
Taste		☆ ☆ ☆ ☆ ☆
Finish		☆ ☆ ☆ ☆ ☆

Pairs With	Serving Temperature

Notes

Ratings ☆ ☆ ☆ ☆ ☆

Wine Name ______________________

Winery ____________ Region ____________

Grapes ____________ Vintage ____________ Alcohol % ________

Appearance		☆ ☆ ☆ ☆ ☆
Aroma		☆ ☆ ☆ ☆ ☆
Body		☆ ☆ ☆ ☆ ☆
Taste		☆ ☆ ☆ ☆ ☆
Finish		☆ ☆ ☆ ☆ ☆

Pairs With	Serving Temperature

Notes

Ratings ☆ ☆ ☆ ☆ ☆

Wine Name ______

Winery ______ Region ______

Grapes ______ Vintage ______ Alcohol % ______

Appearance		☆ ☆ ☆ ☆ ☆
Aroma		☆ ☆ ☆ ☆ ☆
Body		☆ ☆ ☆ ☆ ☆
Taste		☆ ☆ ☆ ☆ ☆
Finish		☆ ☆ ☆ ☆ ☆

Pairs With	Serving Temperature

Notes

Ratings ☆ ☆ ☆ ☆ ☆

Wine Name ______________________

Winery ____________ Region ____________

Grapes ____________ Vintage ____________ Alcohol % ________

Appearance		☆ ☆ ☆ ☆ ☆
Aroma		☆ ☆ ☆ ☆ ☆
Body		☆ ☆ ☆ ☆ ☆
Taste		☆ ☆ ☆ ☆ ☆
Finish		☆ ☆ ☆ ☆ ☆

Pairs With	Serving Temperature

Notes

Ratings ☆ ☆ ☆ ☆ ☆

Wine Name ______________________

Winery ______________ Region ______________

Grapes ______________ Vintage ______________ Alcohol % ________

Appearance		☆ ☆ ☆ ☆ ☆
Aroma		☆ ☆ ☆ ☆ ☆
Body		☆ ☆ ☆ ☆ ☆
Taste		☆ ☆ ☆ ☆ ☆
Finish		☆ ☆ ☆ ☆ ☆

Pairs With	Serving Temperature

Notes

Ratings ☆ ☆ ☆ ☆ ☆

Wine Name ______________________

Winery ____________ Region ____________

Grapes ____________ Vintage ____________ Alcohol % ________

Appearance		☆ ☆ ☆ ☆ ☆
Aroma		☆ ☆ ☆ ☆ ☆
Body		☆ ☆ ☆ ☆ ☆
Taste		☆ ☆ ☆ ☆ ☆
Finish		☆ ☆ ☆ ☆ ☆

Pairs With	Serving Temperature

Notes

Ratings ☆ ☆ ☆ ☆ ☆

Wine Name ______________________________

Winery ______________ Region ______________

Grapes ______________ Vintage ______________ Alcohol % __________

Appearance		☆ ☆ ☆ ☆ ☆
Aroma		☆ ☆ ☆ ☆ ☆
Body		☆ ☆ ☆ ☆ ☆
Taste		☆ ☆ ☆ ☆ ☆
Finish		☆ ☆ ☆ ☆ ☆

Pairs With	Serving Temperature

Notes

Ratings ☆ ☆ ☆ ☆ ☆

Wine Name ____________________

Winery ____________ Region ____________

Grapes ____________ Vintage ____________ Alcohol % ________

Appearance		☆ ☆ ☆ ☆ ☆
Aroma		☆ ☆ ☆ ☆ ☆
Body		☆ ☆ ☆ ☆ ☆
Taste		☆ ☆ ☆ ☆ ☆
Finish		☆ ☆ ☆ ☆ ☆

Pairs With	Serving Temperature

Notes

Ratings ☆ ☆ ☆ ☆ ☆

Wine Name ____________________

Winery ____________ Region ____________

Grapes ____________ Vintage ____________ Alcohol % ________

Appearance		☆ ☆ ☆ ☆ ☆
Aroma		☆ ☆ ☆ ☆ ☆
Body		☆ ☆ ☆ ☆ ☆
Taste		☆ ☆ ☆ ☆ ☆
Finish		☆ ☆ ☆ ☆ ☆

Pairs With	Serving Temperature

Notes

Ratings ☆ ☆ ☆ ☆ ☆

Wine Name ______________________

Winery ______________ Region ______________

Grapes ______________ Vintage ______________ Alcohol % ________

Appearance		☆ ☆ ☆ ☆ ☆
Aroma		☆ ☆ ☆ ☆ ☆
Body		☆ ☆ ☆ ☆ ☆
Taste		☆ ☆ ☆ ☆ ☆
Finish		☆ ☆ ☆ ☆ ☆

Pairs With	Serving Temperature

Notes

Ratings ☆ ☆ ☆ ☆ ☆

Wine Name ______________________

Winery ______________ Region ______________

Grapes ______________ Vintage ______________ Alcohol % __________

Appearance		☆ ☆ ☆ ☆ ☆
Aroma		☆ ☆ ☆ ☆ ☆
Body		☆ ☆ ☆ ☆ ☆
Taste		☆ ☆ ☆ ☆ ☆
Finish		☆ ☆ ☆ ☆ ☆

Pairs With	Serving Temperature

Notes

Ratings ☆ ☆ ☆ ☆ ☆

Wine Name

Winery ______ Region ______

Grapes ______ Vintage ______ Alcohol % ______

Appearance		☆ ☆ ☆ ☆ ☆
Aroma		☆ ☆ ☆ ☆ ☆
Body		☆ ☆ ☆ ☆ ☆
Taste		☆ ☆ ☆ ☆ ☆
Finish		☆ ☆ ☆ ☆ ☆

Pairs With	Serving Temperature

Notes

Ratings ☆ ☆ ☆ ☆ ☆

Wine Name ______________________

Winery ______________ Region ______________

Grapes ______________ Vintage ______________ Alcohol % __________

Appearance		☆ ☆ ☆ ☆ ☆
Aroma		☆ ☆ ☆ ☆ ☆
Body		☆ ☆ ☆ ☆ ☆
Taste		☆ ☆ ☆ ☆ ☆
Finish		☆ ☆ ☆ ☆ ☆

Pairs With	Serving Temperature

Notes

Ratings ☆ ☆ ☆ ☆ ☆

Wine Name ______________________

Winery ____________ Region ____________

Grapes ____________ Vintage ____________ Alcohol % ________

Appearance		☆ ☆ ☆ ☆ ☆
Aroma		☆ ☆ ☆ ☆ ☆
Body		☆ ☆ ☆ ☆ ☆
Taste		☆ ☆ ☆ ☆ ☆
Finish		☆ ☆ ☆ ☆ ☆

Pairs With	Serving Temperature

Notes

Ratings ☆ ☆ ☆ ☆ ☆

Wine Name ______

Winery ______ Region ______

Grapes ______ Vintage ______ Alcohol % ______

Appearance		☆ ☆ ☆ ☆ ☆
Aroma		☆ ☆ ☆ ☆ ☆
Body		☆ ☆ ☆ ☆ ☆
Taste		☆ ☆ ☆ ☆ ☆
Finish		☆ ☆ ☆ ☆ ☆

Pairs With	Serving Temperature

Notes

Ratings ☆ ☆ ☆ ☆ ☆

Wine Name

Winery ____________ Region ____________

Grapes ____________ Vintage ____________ Alcohol % ____________

Appearance		☆ ☆ ☆ ☆ ☆
Aroma		☆ ☆ ☆ ☆ ☆
Body		☆ ☆ ☆ ☆ ☆
Taste		☆ ☆ ☆ ☆ ☆
Finish		☆ ☆ ☆ ☆ ☆

Pairs With	Serving Temperature

Notes

Ratings ☆ ☆ ☆ ☆ ☆

Wine Name ____________________

Winery ____________ Region ____________

Grapes ____________ Vintage ____________ Alcohol % ________

Appearance		☆ ☆ ☆ ☆ ☆
Aroma		☆ ☆ ☆ ☆ ☆
Body		☆ ☆ ☆ ☆ ☆
Taste		☆ ☆ ☆ ☆ ☆
Finish		☆ ☆ ☆ ☆ ☆

Pairs With	Serving Temperature

Notes

Ratings ☆ ☆ ☆ ☆ ☆

Wine Name ______________________

Winery ______________ Region ______________

Grapes ______________ Vintage ______________ Alcohol % ________

Appearance		☆ ☆ ☆ ☆ ☆
Aroma		☆ ☆ ☆ ☆ ☆
Body		☆ ☆ ☆ ☆ ☆
Taste		☆ ☆ ☆ ☆ ☆
Finish		☆ ☆ ☆ ☆ ☆

Pairs With	Serving Temperature

Notes

Ratings ☆ ☆ ☆ ☆ ☆

Wine Name ______________________________

Winery ____________ Region ____________

Grapes ____________ Vintage ____________ Alcohol % ________

Appearance		☆ ☆ ☆ ☆ ☆
Aroma		☆ ☆ ☆ ☆ ☆
Body		☆ ☆ ☆ ☆ ☆
Taste		☆ ☆ ☆ ☆ ☆
Finish		☆ ☆ ☆ ☆ ☆

Pairs With	Serving Temperature

Notes

Ratings ☆ ☆ ☆ ☆ ☆

Wine Name

Winery ____________ Region ____________

Grapes ____________ Vintage ____________ Alcohol % ____________

Appearance		☆ ☆ ☆ ☆ ☆
Aroma		☆ ☆ ☆ ☆ ☆
Body		☆ ☆ ☆ ☆ ☆
Taste		☆ ☆ ☆ ☆ ☆
Finish		☆ ☆ ☆ ☆ ☆

Pairs With	Serving Temperature

Notes

Ratings ☆ ☆ ☆ ☆ ☆

Wine Name ______________________

Winery ____________ Region ____________

Grapes ____________ Vintage ____________ Alcohol % ________

Appearance		☆ ☆ ☆ ☆ ☆
Aroma		☆ ☆ ☆ ☆ ☆
Body		☆ ☆ ☆ ☆ ☆
Taste		☆ ☆ ☆ ☆ ☆
Finish		☆ ☆ ☆ ☆ ☆

Pairs With	Serving Temperature

Notes

Ratings ☆ ☆ ☆ ☆ ☆

Wine Name

Winery ______ Region ______

Grapes ______ Vintage ______ Alcohol % ______

Appearance		☆ ☆ ☆ ☆ ☆
Aroma		☆ ☆ ☆ ☆ ☆
Body		☆ ☆ ☆ ☆ ☆
Taste		☆ ☆ ☆ ☆ ☆
Finish		☆ ☆ ☆ ☆ ☆

Pairs With	Serving Temperature

Notes

Ratings ☆ ☆ ☆ ☆ ☆

Wine Name ____________________

Winery ____________ Region ____________

Grapes ____________ Vintage ____________ Alcohol % ________

Appearance		☆ ☆ ☆ ☆ ☆
Aroma		☆ ☆ ☆ ☆ ☆
Body		☆ ☆ ☆ ☆ ☆
Taste		☆ ☆ ☆ ☆ ☆
Finish		☆ ☆ ☆ ☆ ☆

Pairs With	Serving Temperature

Notes

Ratings ☆ ☆ ☆ ☆ ☆

Wine Name

Winery ______ Region ______

Grapes ______ Vintage ______ Alcohol % ______

Appearance		☆ ☆ ☆ ☆ ☆
Aroma		☆ ☆ ☆ ☆ ☆
Body		☆ ☆ ☆ ☆ ☆
Taste		☆ ☆ ☆ ☆ ☆
Finish		☆ ☆ ☆ ☆ ☆

Pairs With	Serving Temperature

Notes

Ratings ☆ ☆ ☆ ☆ ☆

Wine Name

Winery ______________ Region ______________

Grapes ______________ Vintage ______________ Alcohol % ______________

Appearance		☆ ☆ ☆ ☆ ☆
Aroma		☆ ☆ ☆ ☆ ☆
Body		☆ ☆ ☆ ☆ ☆
Taste		☆ ☆ ☆ ☆ ☆
Finish		☆ ☆ ☆ ☆ ☆

Pairs With	Serving Temperature

Notes

Ratings ☆ ☆ ☆ ☆ ☆

Wine Name

Winery ________ Region ________

Grapes ________ Vintage ________ Alcohol % ________

Appearance		☆ ☆ ☆ ☆ ☆
Aroma		☆ ☆ ☆ ☆ ☆
Body		☆ ☆ ☆ ☆ ☆
Taste		☆ ☆ ☆ ☆ ☆
Finish		☆ ☆ ☆ ☆ ☆

Pairs With	Serving Temperature

Notes

Ratings ☆ ☆ ☆ ☆ ☆

Wine Name

Winery ______ Region ______

Grapes ______ Vintage ______ Alcohol % ______

Appearance		☆ ☆ ☆ ☆ ☆
Aroma		☆ ☆ ☆ ☆ ☆
Body		☆ ☆ ☆ ☆ ☆
Taste		☆ ☆ ☆ ☆ ☆
Finish		☆ ☆ ☆ ☆ ☆

Pairs With	Serving Temperature

Notes

Ratings ☆ ☆ ☆ ☆ ☆

Wine Name ______________________

Winery ______________ Region ______________

Grapes ______________ Vintage ______________ Alcohol % __________

Appearance		☆ ☆ ☆ ☆ ☆
Aroma		☆ ☆ ☆ ☆ ☆
Body		☆ ☆ ☆ ☆ ☆
Taste		☆ ☆ ☆ ☆ ☆
Finish		☆ ☆ ☆ ☆ ☆

Pairs With	Serving Temperature

Notes

Ratings ☆ ☆ ☆ ☆ ☆

Wine Name ______________________

Winery ______________ Region ______________

Grapes ______________ Vintage ______________ Alcohol % __________

Appearance		☆ ☆ ☆ ☆ ☆
Aroma		☆ ☆ ☆ ☆ ☆
Body		☆ ☆ ☆ ☆ ☆
Taste		☆ ☆ ☆ ☆ ☆
Finish		☆ ☆ ☆ ☆ ☆

Pairs With	Serving Temperature

Notes

Ratings ☆ ☆ ☆ ☆ ☆

Printed by Amazon Italia Logistica S.r.l.
Torrazza Piemonte (TO), Italy

11616772R00089